I am
Adorie

To order additional copies of this book, contact:
Xlibris
844-714-8691
www.Xlibris.com
Orders@Xlibris.com

ISBN: Softcover   978-1-6641-8608-8
        EBook   978-1-6641-8607-1

Print information available on the last page

Rev. date: 07/20/2021

I am
Adorie

ODARRIE JACKSON

Twice lives virtuous—Mary and I, Adorie, forever live immaculate.

Today lives Adorie.

I am the reflection of God's Glory.

I am not just my father's Daughter.

I am source from the author of creation, emblem of completion, evidence of perfection.

I am Adorie; there is only one me.

I am divine. How can I follow the traditions or let the routine of the Cornals, the Sadamites, or the worlians lead me?

Our nature and purpose are different. Therefore, all I ever wanted and will ever need is within me. The divine Leadeth me.

I am a woman, virtuous and Pure. My nature defines it. My way of life explains it. Restoring morals and serving of wisdom is the proof of it. Ordained by God, I am Adorie.

I am who I am from divine existence.

I am above and beyond your words.

I am Adorie; understanding is one with me.

Divine knowledge upholds and wisdom comforts me.

Great I am today. Yet, better I shall be tomorrow as I learn more about myself. Wisdom leadeth me.

Therefore, before you speak remember that I am a reflection of you. What you say about me is not necessarily true; it may be just your view. Halfway down is also halfway up.

The dog says *ruff-ruff*. The cat says *meow*. By nature they are different, yet beautiful in their own way.

What is my vision? My destiny?

My purpose?

You can't tell it! now I tell you, Endless possibilities I am!

I am EVERYTHING, not limited to anything. I will be the best at whatever I do.

The best is yet to come because through me, God's will shall be done.

As the trees go through the process of producing fruits, so shall I, Adorie, go through the process of producing the Divine workings and Purpose of Human beings, Healing Hearts, Bodies, and Minds, Restoring Souls, Tranquility, and Love.

I am Solitude, Tranquility, Peace, Hope, and Possibilities.

I am the Solution, the Resource, the Restorer, mental revolutionist, the Successor, the Answer, the way, the light.

I am one with God.

Nothing now, to come, or in the past can change that.

So, never forget that the Divine is within me; I am Adorie.

I, Adorie, give praises to God Almighty.

Yes, you heard me; I give praise to God Almighty.

As water and sun is   life to plants so is my heavenly father everlasting life to me. Therefore, I am forever in the midst of power and glory as I am within the Almighty. Amen.

Adorie,

You are my Savior, my Restorer, and my Deliverer. The best of me, the Divine of me, the Remnant of the remnant of me, the Purest part of me. You're the voice of God to me. Daughter of our heavenly father God Almighty. I, Odarrie, love you, Adorie Bella Jackson, now and forever. Never forget or doubt who you are.

Interpretation of Drawings

Seed—words

Earth—mind

Seed in the earth—mind open to accept the word **Dark clouds with rain**—words of truth and correction

Sunshine—warm love of parents and genuinely positive people who mean well

Chrubs—negative people, bullies, and manipulators

The blossom—the beauty of character

The roots—the core and foundation of Being

The spring—God sustaining Power

Tree with fruits—living to the highest potential

Tree with ripe fruits—result of living to the highest potential, being the truly divine that you are, restoring delivering, and strengthening all that has life

Printed in the United States
by Baker & Taylor Publisher Services